Dr. Jamoke's Little Book of Hitherto

Uncompiled Facts and Curiosities

Regarding Bees

Other Titles from

New London Librarium

Dr. Jamoke's Little Book of Hitherto Uncompiled Facts and Curiosities Regarding Bees

by
Hezekiah Jamoke
with
Glenn Alan Cheney

New London Librarium

Dr. Jamoke's Little Book of Hitherto Uncompiled
Facts and Curiosities Regarding Bees
by Hezekiah Jamoke, with Glenn Alan Cheney

Cover art by
Kathleen Boushee (bees) and Colleen Hennessey (flowers)

Copyright © 2016 Glenn Alan Cheney

Published by
New London Librarium
P.O. Box 284
Hanover, CT 06350
NLLibrarium.com

ISBN-13: 978-1537414041

ISBN-10: 1537414046

Printed in the United States

For Solange and Terri

Contents

Gods, Goddesses,
Nymphs, Saints,
& Suspicions

Your Lord revealed to the bees: 'Build dwellings in the mountains and the trees, and also in the structures which men erect. Then eat from every kind of fruit and travel the paths of your Lord, which have been made easy for you to follow.' From inside them comes a drink of varying colors, containing healing for mankind. There is certainly a Sign in that for people who reflect.

Qur'an, 16:69

My son, eat thou honey, because it is good; and the honey-comb, which is sweet to thy taste: So shall the knowledge of wisdom be unto thy soul: when thou hast found it, then there shall be a reward, and thy expectation shall not be cut off.

Proverbs 24:13-14

The tears of the Egyptian god Ra became bees as they fell.

The Egyptian goddess Nut could manifest herself as a bee, and for all anybody knows, she still can.

Bubilas and Austeéja were the Lithuanian god and goddess of bees.

Bhramari was the Hindu god of bees.

Colel Cab was the Mayan goddess of bees.

Samson, of Biblical fame, was not only strong but clever, and honeybees came to play a part in an interesting event. Samson, it seems, had seen the woman of his dreams, but she was from among the uncircumcised Philistines who ruled over Israel. He took his parents to meet her. Along the way, he encountered a lion in a vineyard. He tore the lion apart with his bare hands, though apparently the altercation didn't create enough noise for his parents to hear. He never told them about it.

They met the girl, and, according to the King James version, "She pleased him well." He came back later and married her. On his way home, he looked for the carcass of the lion. He found it full of bees and honey! He dug right in, ate some, and took some home to his parents, though he never told them or his wife where he got it.

Later, he took his father to see his new wife. As was customary, he held a feast for his Philistine family. Thirty uncircumcised men were assigned to be his groomsmen. They befriended him. But not a lot. Sampson offered them a cruel riddle and told them that if they answered it in seven days, he would give all thirty of them a set of sheets and garments. But if they failed to answer it, they would have to give him thirty sheets and as many garments.

The offer was undoubtedly both intriguing and disturbing, but they agreed. And Samson said unto them, "Out of the eater came something to eat, and out of the strong came something sweet."

They couldn't figure it out. Desperate, they asked his wife to tease it out of him. His wife cried for a week and "lay sore upon him." She said, "You do but hate me, and love me not: you have put forth a riddle to the children of my people, and have not told it me."

Samson, nagged raw, finally told her, and she told them. And they told Samson the answer. And Samson said, "If you had not plowed with my heifer, you would not have solved my riddle."

The Bible does not mention how the wife felt about being called a heifer or exactly what Samson meant by "plowed," but it didn't matter because that marriage was effectively over. Samson, infused with the spirit of the Lord, went and killed 30 uncircumcised Philistines and took their garments.

And his wife? She was given to one of Samson's groomsmen. End of story? Certainly not. It got even more complicated. But that's the end of the part that involved bees.

13

The Talmud is very specific about how big a beehive one may throw in the street without culpability. It's not as simple as one might think. For a while it was believed that if it was less than six spans (that is, six hand-widths) wide, the thrower was culpable. If wider than that, it was not a Talmudic problem. But upon further thought, it was decided that if the hive is thrown with its mouth down and it's a trifle over seven spans high (as opposed to wide), the verdict is *guilty*.

Nothing in the Talmud *requires* the throwing of beehives into the street, and local ordinances may take precedence over the Talmud, so Dr. Jamoke's advice is: *Just don't*.

Mellona was the Roman goddess of bees. Her name derived from the Greek Melisseus of Crete, the "Bee Man" whose daughters (one named Melissa) hid the infant Zeus when his father, Cronus, was coming to eat him. The daughters hid the babe in a cave and nursed him with goat milk and honey. When four men discovered them, bees chased the mwn away. For this favor, the bees were rewarded with the gift of asexual reproduction. When Cronus found out that Melissa had thwarted his brephophagous repast, he turned her into an earthworm. Zeus, still enjoying milk and honey atop Mt. Olympus, rescued her by turning her into a bee.

Potnia, the Mistress Goddess of the Minoan-Mycenaeans, also known as "The Pure Mother Bee," named her priestesses Melissae, or bees, after Melissa, an elderly priestess of Demeter, the goddess of agriculture and harvest. When Melissa refused to tell other women her priestly secrets, they tore her to pieces. Demeter avenged her by causing a plague of bees to rise from her body.

Deborah is Hebrew for *bee*. Deborah's parentsmay have named her that for the desirable qualities of the bee: hard-working, unselfish, untiring, intelligent, and with a sting for her enemies. Deborah grew up true to her name, becoming a prophetess and the only female judge of the Israelites. She rendered her judgments and prophecies beneath a palm tree. Her army of 10,000 men defeated an enemy force that included 900 iron chariots. Like most hard-working female bees, she never bore a child.

Dubious Wisdom

When bees to distance wing their flight
Days are warm and skies are bright
But when their flight ends near their home
Stormy weather is sure to come.

From beavers,
bees should learn to mend their ways.
A bee works;
a beaver works and plays.

A swarm of bees in May
is worth a load of hay;
A swarm of bees in June
is worth a silver spoon.
a swarm of bees in July
is not worth a fly.

No bees,
no honey.
No work,
no money.

When you shoot an arrow of truth, dip its point in honey.

Arab Proverb

Where the honey, there the bees.

Latin Proverb

One bee is better than a handful of flies.

English Proverb

Bees that hae honey in their mouths hae stings in their tails.

Scottish Proverb

A man doesn't escape from bees with a lump of honey in his hand.

African Proverb

Bees do not become hornets.

Spanish Proverb

Bees touch no fading flowers.

French Proverb

The buzzing of flies does not turn them into bees.

Georgian Proverb

To be rich with bees and mares is to be rich and have
nothing.

Sicilian Proverb

Three things you cannot comprehend: the mind of a woman, the working of the bees, and the ebb and flow of the
tide.

Irish Proverb

He who would steal honey must not be afraid of bees.

Danish Proverb

Boys avoid the bees that stung them.

German Proverb

Not a single bee has ever sent you an invoice. And that is
part of the problem—because most of what comes to us
from nature is free, because it is not invoiced, because it
is not priced, because it is not traded in markets, we tend
to ignore it.

Pavan Sukhde

The bee is more honored than animals not because she labors but because she labors for others.

St. John Chrysostom

I don't like to hear cut-and-dried sermons. No, when I hear a man preach, I like to see him act as if he were fighting bees.

Abraham Lincoln

Every saint has a bee in his halo.

Elbert Hubbard

That which is not good for the beehive is not good for the bees.

Marcus Aurelius

Everything takes time. Bees have to move very fast to stay still.

David Foster Wallace

If bees disappeared off the face of the earth, man would have only four years to live.

Maurice Maeterlinck

Handle a book as a bee does a flower. Extract its sweetness but do not damage it.

John Muir

The keeping of bees is like the direction of sunbeams.

Henry David Thoreau

In the village, a sage should go about like a bee, which, not harming flower, color, or scent, flies off with the nectar.

Anonymous

To be successful, one has to be one of three bees: the queen bee, the hardest working bee, or the bee that does not fit in.

Suzy Kassem

For better or worse, honey bees are often much too busy to be bothered with personal reflection.

Susan Brackney

We think we can make honey without sharing in the fate of bees, but we are in truth nothing but poor bees, destined to accomplish our task and then die.

Muriel Barbery

Hope is the only bee that makes honey without flowers.

Robert Green Ingersoll

• In Central Europe, a bride-to-be will walk her groom past a beehive to test his faithfulness. If a bee stings him, the marriage is best called off.

• The Vikings believed that mead mixed with the blood of Kvasir created the Mead of Poetry. Whoever drank it would receive the gifts of poetry, wisdom, and immortality.

• The ancient Greeks considered bees "the birds of muse." They were also considered souls of the dead in transit between death and the next world.

• Ancient Greeks dabbed honey on lips of babies to promote eloquence and song—ideally even prophecy.

• If a bee landed on an ancient sleeping Greek child's lips, the child would become a poet or, at the very least, incapable of speaking or writing anything other than truth. Such was the fate of Plato, Pindar, and St. Ambrose, the saint of beekeepers,

• In the British Isles it is believed that bees hum a special hymn on Christmas Eve.

• In ancient Egypt, the bee represented the pharaoh's sovereignty over Lower Egypt.

• The Egyptian Temple of Neith, goddess of the night, was known as "The House of the Bee."

• The Sanctuary of Osiris, god of the underworld and death, was "The Mansion of the Bee."

• There was a time when people believed the queen bee was a king.

• In Poland, Michel Wiscionsky was chosen king because bees landed on him during the election.

• In ancient Lithuania, Austeja was the bee goddess. Her husband, Bablilos, was the bee god.

• Hindus believe in Madhu-Vidya, the "Wisdom that Reveals Delight," or "Secret Honey" of the Creative Spirit or the Absolute. Madhu is Sanskrit for "honey." The word comes from the same Indo-European root as mead.

• In Britain and Ireland it was believed that if a bumblebee buzzed around your house or window, a visitor was coming. If anyone killed the bee, the visitor would bring bad news.

• In Wales it was believed that if bees made a home near yours, you would be prosperous. If a bee landed on your hand, you'd have good luck. If a bumblebee died in your home, it meant bad luck.

• A bumblebee on an English ship meant good luck.

• Lethargic bees augur misfortune; busy bees, good fortune.

• If you dream of getting stung by a bee, you will be betrayed by someone you know.

• In Britain, bees were invited to weddings and funerals, and if they didn't come, a piece of the wedding or wake cake was left at their hive.

• In England, a girl could prove her virginity by walking through a swarm of bees without getting stung.

History

The ancient names beginning with "Mel-" (Mellona, Melissa, Melisseus, etc.) go back to the Greek word *melitta*, bee, which descended into such words as mellitology (the study of bees), melliferous (producing honey), mellifluous (sounding smooth, like honey), and words meaning honey in other languages, such as *miel* (Spanish and French), *mel* (Portuguese), *miele* (Italian), *meli* (Corsican), *miere* (Romanian), мед (Russian), and *siwo myèl* (Haitian Creole).

Before there were beekeepers, bee hunters roamed the earth. As long as 25,000 years ago they were drawing pictures of the hunt on rocks in Spain, India, Australia, and southern Africa. The Cueva de la Araña in Valencia features drawings from 10,000 years ago depicting honey collection, bee swarms, and men on ladders to get at hives.

Medieval doctors recommended pouring honey in the ear to treat ear ailments. If honey didn't work—and it wasn't necessarily the first thing to try—other recommended ear douches included oil, vinegar, bile of rabbits and pigs, human milk, eggs of ants in onion juice, smoked seven-day-old goat urine, horse urine, warm water with entrails of spiders, and eel fat. None of these treatments are recommended by modern medicine, not even the goat urine, not even the honey. Not even on an in-law.

The queen bee was once presumed to be useless for she had no way to carry pollen, her tongue was too short to lap up nectar, and she could not produce wax. This apparent uselessness led Aristotle to conclude she was a king, not a queen.

Propolis, also known as bee glue, comes from the Greek *pro*, meaning *in the front of* and *polis*, meaning *city*.

Propolis has been used for medicinal purposes since at least 300 BC. The gummy, intensely flavorful substance was used by ancient Greek, Roman, Arab, and Incan physicians. Egyptians used it to embalm mummies. It is vaguely and uncertainly referred to in the Bible as balm and balsam.

Antonio Stradivari is believed to have used propolis as a varnish on his violins, some of which are over 300 years old.

No one knows when the first honey bees were brought from Europe to the New World, but it was certainly in the days when it took a sailing ship two months or more to make the crossing. The bees had to be confined the whole time. Since ships avoided sailing in the winter, when ice could ruin sails, the bees were awake and lively during the whole trip. They couldn't be released because as soon as the ship sailed a few feet, they'd never find their way back to the hive. When they finally reached the New World, they, like the passengers, were no doubt itching to see a flower.

Pre-Columbian Americans had no *Apis mellifera,* but they cultivated the *Apis melipona*. The melipona was a stingless bee, but a colony produced only a kilo of honey in a year, one-fiftieth that of the mellifera. Cortés made an interesting observation about the Americans of Cozumel, Mexico, in 1519:

> The only trade which the Indians have is in bee hives, and our Procurators will bear to Your Highness specimens of the honey and the bee hives that you may commend them to be examined.

Archeologists later determined that the Maya had been cultivating bees since about 300 BC. They had a bee god named Ah Mucan Cab. In modern times, peasants in Yucatán were using the same means to raise bees that the ancient Egyptians had used: hollow logs stacked on a rack.

April 28, 2013, was a big day for bees and beekeepers, at least in Europe. On that day, the European Union voted to ban neonicotinoid pesticides, which are deadly to bees, for at least two years. But with stiff corporate and agricultural resistance, only 15 of 27 voting nations voted for the ban. Opposition alleged weak science, the need for pesticides, and other possible explanations for a decline in bee populations, including climate change, disease, and loss of habitat.

Bees have less reason to celebrate in the United States, where neonicotinoids are still used, and 44 percent of all hives died in the winter of 2015-16. The next spring, pro-bee activists delivered 2.6 million dead bees to the U.S. Congress. But it takes more than 2.6 million dead bees to motivate Congress. There was no legislative response.

Aristotle, Plato, Virgil, Seneca, Erasmus, Shakespeare, Marx, and Tolstoy all considered the possibility that bee society might be a model for human society.

Said the ancient Greek Pappus: "Bees...by virtue of a certain geometrical forethought, knew that the hexagon is greater than the square and the triangle and will hold more honey for the same expenditure of material."

Gaius Plinius Secondus (23 AD - 79 AD), more commonly known as Pliny the Elder, author of *Naturalis Historia*, a set of 37 volumes that attempted to record the entire knowledge of the Roman Empire, described migratory beekeeping along the River Po in the 1st century AD. Hives were tubes of pottery, wicker, or wood that could be loaded on pack animals and boats. When food for bees was lacking in the immediate neighborhood, the inhabitants put their hives in boats and took them, by night, five miles upstream. The bees emerged at dawn, fed and by end of day returned to the boats. They changed the position of the boats until they sat low in the water under the weight of the honey. Then the boats were taken back and the honey harvested.

The same was done in ancient Egypt, where beekeeper petitions on papyrus requested that hives be moved by donkey instead of boat due to flooding.

Bees arrived in North America on ships from Europe. They moved west at about the same pace as settlers. By 1811, they were 600 miles up the Missouri River. By then, Indians already recognized bees as a bad harbinger. Wherever they were found, white settlers were soon to follow.

Rev. Charles Butler (1560-1647), a.k.a. the Father of English Beekeeping, a logician, grammarist, author, and Vicar of Wootton St. Lawrence, beekeeper, and author of The Feminine Monarchie (i.e. the queen bee) said: "The Drone which is a gross hive-bee without sting, has been alwaies reputed for a sluggard, and that worthily: for howsoever he brave it with his round velvet cappe, his side gown, his great paunch, and his lowd voice, yet is he but an idle person living by the sweat of others' brows. For he worketh not at al, ether at home or abroad, and yet spendeth as much as two labourers; you shal never finde his maw without a good drop of the purest nectar." Butler also spoke out against the inconsistency in spelling in the English language.

NATURE

The study of bees is melittology.

The honey bee is classified thus:

Kingdom: *Animalia* (because they are multicellular, can move of their own volition, and ingest organisms or their products)

Phylum: *Arthropoda* (because they have an exoskeletons and no spines, segmented bodies with a pair of joined appendages for each segment)

Class: *Insecta* (because they have compound eyes, two antennae, three body sections, one of which is a thorax with a pair of legs on each of three thoracic sections.

Order: *Hymenoptera* (because they have membranous (*hymen*) wings (*ptera*)

Family: *Apidae* (because it's a bee)

Subfamily: *Apinae* (because it has a pollen basket)

Genus: *Apis* (Latin for bee)

Species: *Apis mellifera* (from the Greek, *meli*, meaning honey, and the Latin, *fero*, meaning carry.

Officially—that is, nomenclaturally—*honey bee* should be two words, though less picky dictionaries tend to recognize *honeybee* as a word. The Integrated Taxonomic Information System of the Entomological Society of America, lists the *Apis mellifera* as "honey bee." The term isn't like *dragonfly* and *butterfly*, which are each one word because they aren't flies.

The genus Apis can be divided into three branches based on how they nest.

Open nest bees: *Apis dorsata* and *Apis laboriosa*

Dwarf, single-comb bees: *Apis florae* and *Apis andreniformis*

Cavity nest bees: *Apis cerana, Apis koschevnikovi, Apis nuluensis, Apis nigrocincta,* and *Apis mellifera.*

Bees are found throughout North America, from Arctic Alaska to tropical Florida and southern Mexico. They live in deserts, forests, meadows, and cities. The only places free of bees are the tops of high mountains.

Of the 20,000 species of bees in the world, about 4,000 species are native to North America.

The honey bee isn't one of the natives.

Honey bees forage from morning until evening. (Beekeepers often orient the hive opening to the east so the early sun shines in the door, all the sooner to tell the bees it's time to get to work.) Bees can remember what time higher food sources were available on a previous day, so on the subsequent day, they will forage more at that time. They generally spend less than five minutes at a foraging site.

Busy as a bee? Which bee? How about busy as bee researchers at the University of Illinois who set up five hives, each with about 2,000 day-old bees. They fastened tiny transponders to a bunch of the bees so they could count, with scanners, how many were going out to forage. They found that 20 percent of a hive's bees accounted for 50 percent of the foraging activity. In other words, there were a lot of less-busy bees. When the scientists killed a number of bees who had been going out to forage, other bees were replacing them within a day. Whether the less-active bees were lazy, occupied with indoor activities such as housekeeping and child-rearing, or just held back for emergencies was not determined. In any event, not all bees are as busy as beavers.

Pre-adult honey bees raised in high-aggression environments were found to be 10-15 percent more aggressive as adults. However, unlike humans and many other animals, the socially induced high aggression made the bees more resilient rather than less resilient to immune stressors such as, in the bees, neonicotinoid pesticides. Humans raised under high aggression would be more, not less, likely to suffer health problems.

Bees' lives are measured in days, not years. During the first three days of a bee's life, a worker bee is a chamber maid cleaning brood cells, but she will spend 20 percent of her day resting and 20 percent walking around. After age four, as her hypopharyngeal glands start secreting brood food, she becomes a nurse. By age 12, she knows how to sting and she goes to work in food storage, evaporating nectar to make it honey, packing pollen, building comb, and helping guard the hive entrance. At age 20, she's ready for dangerous work outside the hive, gathering pollen, nectar, water, and resin. By the time she's 28, she has worn her wings ragged and worked herself to death.

Isopentyl acetate (a.k.a. amyl acetate) is one of two alarm pheromones a honey bes can emit. She does so under two circumstances: when she takse a stinging posture, typically on the hive's front porch (tail raised and pointed outward, wings buzzing viciously), and when her stinger is ripped from her body. The alarm pheromone alerts other bees and hails guards to the entrance. But not all available bees show up to guard. Why not? One study determined that it might be a matter of individual personality.

The queen of the Arctic bumblebee *(Bombus polaris)* wears a thick coat and leads a hard life. Her workers die come winter. For the next nine months, she has to live alone in an almost lifeless torpor in a mouse nest or other underground burrow. She's pregnant the whole time. When the first Arctic poppies, Arctic roses, and Arctic willows blossom in the spring, she has to forage for herself. She warms herself with the exertion. Every day she has to go out for more food. She builds a little nest and a hatching chamber of pollen and wax. She covers the floor with a plug of dust and nectar and therein lays some 20 eggs. She shuts it up with more wax and dust. To keep it warm, she presses her belly to it and quivers her flight muscles. Ten days later, she does it again. By June, she has a colony, but by October, everybody's dead but her.

Africanized honey bees (AHB) cannot be distinguished from the common honey bees of North America with the naked eye. They fly at about the same speed—12-15 mph, depending on urgency. The AHB sting is no worse than that of the European bees most common in the United States. However, in defense of their hive, AHBs are ten times more likely to sting, will meet an attacker farther from the hive, and will chase him, her, or it a quarter mile or more.

The smallest bee, *Perdita minima*, is half the size of the eye of its largest cousin, the carpenter bee (*Xylocopa varipuncta*).

Honey bees flap their wings 230 times per second when hovering.

Flies have just one pair of wings; bees have two.

When a bee consumes nectar from a flower, she swallows it into a "honey stomach." This organ is not part of the digestive system. It has no exit other than the entrance.

Back at the hive, she regurgitates the nectar repeatedly, taking turns with other worker bees to lap it up and heave it out. This ingestive-regurgitative process, which can take 20 minutes, uses digestive enzymes to hydrolyze the sucrose of the nectar to form a mixture of glucose and fructose. Yes, honey is bee barf...but natural!

Honey bees are excellent pollinators, but since they evolved in Europe, they aren't especially adept at pollinating many North American food crops. Pumpkins, cherries, blueberries, and cranberries are all better pollinated by native bees.

Three-quarters of the fruits, nuts, and vegetables in North America are pollinated by bees. Corn is not one of them. Corn is pollinated by the wind, which is why planting just one row of corn won't lead to much of a crop.

The best bee for pollinating blueberries would be the *Habropoda laboriosa*. And laboriosa she is. Known among friends as the southeastern blueberry bee, she may pay a visit to 50,000 blueberry flowers in her lifetime, lugging around enough pollen to produce 6,000 blueberries—thirty to forty pints.

Matinal bees go out at dawn in search of flowers that bloom in the early hours. Crepuscular bees go out at twilight. Nocturnal bees fly by the light of the moon.

The *Habropoda laboriosa*, like the bumblebee, pollinates through buzz pollination, also known as sonication. Sonication is the only way some flowers can release their pollen, yet the technique is beyond the capability of honey bees. About eight percent of the world's flowers—some 20,000 species—hold their pollen tightly inside their tubular anthers. Among them are those of the eggplant, the potato, the tomato, the blueberry, and the cranberry. Wind might work with a tomato, and with a little luck and elbow grease, a honey bee might knock off a little pollen from berry flowers. But buzz pollinators are better at it. They know how to grab anthers with their jaws and twitch their flight muscles fast enough and hard enough to shake the pollen out of the anther. The action creates a buzz, but it's not the familiar flight buzz. It's more like the sound of a raspberry blown on the belly of a child. It has to be at just the right cycle to cause the pollen to vibrate inside the anther and shoot out the open end.

Bees are herbivores. Wasps, whose ranks include the yellow jacket and the hornet, are carnivores that live off insects or spiders. Wasps came first, appearing in the Jurassic period when the first marine crocodiles were crawling from the sea, pterosaurs ruled the skies, and the first mammals crept meekly in forests of fern.

The life of wasps began to change about 125 million years ago, during the Cretaceous period. Today's continents were all one landmass called Gondwana, where the climate was warm and dry. Flowering plants began to appear. They developed colors and petals that attracted insects, which were better than the wind at pollination. Wasps, hunting for prey in blossoms, discovered the sweetness of nectar and the protein of pollen. Nectar and pollen put up less of a fight than animal prey, so wasps, pursuing an easier, sweeter life, gradually evolved into fuzzier insects with pollen baskets, longer tongues, and colonies adept at storing food for the future, the industrious little buggers we came to know as honey bees.

Some species of bees live independent of a swarm. They reproduce with a mate and raise their brood without the help of others. Other species, including the honey bee and bumblebee, can live only in societies reproduced en masse by a queen and raised by a crew of workers. In that these societal bees cannot survive alone, it can be said that the actual animal isn't the bee—it's the hive as a whole.

Cuckoo bees of various species are not known for their melodious song. Rather, like the cuckoo bird, they lay their eggs in the nests of others. In other words, they are parasites. Some cuckoo bee species kill the larva of their host bee, then insert their own in its place. Tthe larva eats the host's honey, maybe even the host's larva. Cuckoos are so dependent on the efforts of other bees that they have evolved out of their capacity to collect pollen, though they might stop by a flower for a sip of nectar.

Some species of bees have long tongues, others have short tongues. The former, which include honey bees, are adapted for probing into deep flowers. Those with shorter tongues would have to pass up a lily for the shallower florets of a sunflower.

After a queen lays an egg into a comb cell, worker bees pack it with a loaf of nectar, pollen, and spit. The nectar and pollen are food for the larva. The spit prevents bacterial and fungal infection.

The queen bee's stinger is not barbed, enabling her to sting other queens without getting her stinger ripped out, which would cause her death. Other than that, she isn't likely to sting anybody. But she could if she wanted, and more than once.

Queen bees are created at the discretion of worker bees.

The queen bee stays in her hive except to mate, which she may do 15 or 20 times during a single mating flight. She is not a queen in any sense of leadership, power, or privilege. She is more like a slave to those whom she has borne, fulfilling her sole function in life as fast as she can until she weakens, at which point her progeny gather round and kill her with suffocation and heat.

Male bees—the big, fat ones known as drones—have no known function other than sex. Even so, few of them will ever experience it, and those that do tend to have nothing but negative feelings about the brief relationship. Drones do not forage for food, care for the nest, raise the young, or defend the hive. Unlike females, they often leave the hive to take a nap outside. When winter comes, they assume they'll be welcome indoors, but there will be no mating until spring, so who needs them? Nobody. The females haul them outside and toss them over the edge, into the cold.

Drones mate with a queen during her mating flight. A fellow lucky enough to insert his endophallus into the queen and ejaculate therein will, upon retraction, have his endophallus and part of his abdomen ripped out. Sex is fatal to drones.

Bee bread is made by worker bees. The recipe calls for pollen, honey, and a dash of glandular secretion. Tucked into the comb, it ferments. The fermentation releases nutrients from the pollen and creates antibiotics and fatty acids that inhibit spoilage. One job of younger bees is to eat this bee bread, then secrete it through their hypopharynxes. The hypopharynx is a tiny globular gland near the jaw. This secretion is essentially bee spit, but it is known as royal jelly.

All bee larvae are fed a bit of royal jelly to get them going. Then they live on nectar and pollen. However, if workers build a special enlarged cell for a given larva, and pack it with royal jelly, the larva will grow larger and develop ovaries, becoming a queen capable of laying eggs. Humans can manipulate a hive to have more queen cells produced and thus more royal jelly. Royal jelly is typically collected when the larva is four days old. Carefully managed and harvested, a hive can produce a pound or more of royal jelly in a year. A pound of the stuff sells for around $65.00.

Royal jelly is reputed to improve human health, but there is little, if any, scientific evidence of such benefits.

Whenever possible, bees carry waste, including their dead, away from the hive. If, however, a large intruder, such as a mouse, dies in the hive, removal is not an option. The bees will therefore encase the corpse in propolis, embalming it so that it does not rot, stink, or fester. If you were to bite into such a mummy at room temperature, you would find it gummy, and it would stick to your teeth. At cooler temperatures it would be crunchy on the outside, chewy on the inside.

The chemical makeup of propolis varies widely depending on available local plants. The color and content of propolis varies according to local vegetation and time of year. Tree resin, whose function is to seal wounds and prevent infection in trees, is a favorite among bees. In temperate climes, bees look for conifers and poplars. In tropical regions, certain flowers offer banquets of resin. Propolis does for hives what resin does for trees. It seals cracks against intruders and inhibits the growth of bacteria. It also strengthens the hive, secures comb to a frame or other surface, and deters mites.

Propolis is about 50 percent resins and balsam, 30 percent beeswax, 10 percent essential and aromatic oils, five percent pollen, and 5 percent impurities. Among the over 300 botanical chemicals that can be found in propolis, depending on the season and the location of the hive, are lipophilic acaricides, polyprenylated benzophenones, viscidone, naphthoquinone epoxide, prenylated acids, 4-hydroxy-3,5-diprenyl cinnamic acid, sinapinic acid, 3-hydroxy-8,9-dimethoxypterocarpan, medicarpin isoferulic acid, caffeic acid phenethyl ester, chrysin, galangin, and pinocembrin.

A pound of worker bees numbers a little over 3,000 individuals.

A queen bee can lay 2,000 eggs a day.

A hive's bees will fly a total of 40,000 miles to produce a pound of honey.

A pound of honey has about 1,382 calories.

A pound of Honey Nut Cheerios has about 1,680 calories in about 4,160 Cheerios.

Apitoxin is what makes bee stings hurt so much. The most abundant active ingredient in apitoxin is melittin, but the most destructive ingredient is phospholipase A2. Mellitin is the same toxin present in snake venom. Apitoxin is stored in a venom sac that is attached to the stinger. When a bee stings, both stinger and sac are ripped from her abdomen. The stinger in honey bees (and only honey bees) is barbed, so it tends to stay in the victim's skin as the sac continues to pump venom through the stinger into the skin.

An experiment showed that bees, despite having brains no bigger than a sesame seed, can recognize human faces. The bees were presented with photographs of two faces. One face had sucrose in front of it, the other a quinine solution that is bitter to bees. Later, when the reward and punishment were removed, bees tended to go to the face that used to offer a reward. One bee got the "right answer" 93.9% of the time on the first day of training and 75.9% two days later. However, if the photos were turned upside down, performance declined significantly.

One ounce of honey would be enough to fuel a honey bee for a trip around the world. A 7-11 Super Big Gulp™ cup of honey would be enough to get two bees around the world once and then to the moon and back. A Super Big Gulp of Mountain Dew, on the other hand, would most certainly kill them both.

Is altruism genetic? An experiment with bees indicates the possibility.

Bees inherit certain genes from their mother, the queen. These are called matrigenes. Other genes, called patrigenes, are inherited from one of her several mates.

When a queen dies, some worker bees take their sisters' existing eggs and try to nourish them into queens. They don't know which of those eggs come from full sisters who had not only the same mother but the same father, and which had a different father. Odds are about 20:1 an egg carries the genes of a different father. They aren't, in other words, selfishly trying to pass on their own genes.

Other worker bees start to lay their own eggs, though they will inevitably become drones, i.e. males with the genes of their fathers. They aren't, in other words, altruistically doing what's best for the hive. They're doing what's best for propagaing their own DNA.

It turns out that workers who forego laying their own eggs carry matrigenes, while workers who lay their own eggs have the patrigenes.

In other words, genes seem to be directing this altruistic or self-promoting behavior. Matrigenes direct workers to altruistically reproduce someone else's genes for the good of the community. Patrigenes direct workers to pass on their own genes, the ones they inherited from their fathers.

Now the question is: Are there human genes direct people in the same way?

Studies have linked various stressors—pathogens, pesticides, malnutrition—to colony collapse. But scientists still wonder why the collapse sometimes happens so quickly. Two scientists looked into the question by using radio tracking to follow thousands of bees during their entire lifetimes.

They found that in hives under stress, bees went foraging at an earlier age rather than sticking to in-hive tasks until they were two or three weeks old. These "precocious foragers" completed fewer sorties in their lifetimes and died at an earlier age. That disrupted the hive's finely balanced social structure and division of labor. Hives were left with plenty of brood and food but too few adults. Child labor, it seems, is not a good idea even if it seems necessary.

Or maybe it's the manganese. People need a bit of it to stay healthy, but it doesn't take much more to cause people to suffer symptoms like those of Parkinson's disease. Manganese used to be pretty rare, but now it's a common industrial pollutant, so bees end up eating it, too. The same two scientists found that manganese affects bee brains, causing them to grow up sooner and start foraging at a younger age. But they end up making fewer trips to flowers before they die. It's too soon to say whether humans suffer similar symptoms from environmental manganese, but if manganese is harming bees, ultimately it's going to harm people who eat fruits and vegetables pollinated by bees.

Health

Honey should never be given to infants under the age of 12 months due to the possibility of infant botulism. Though most bacteria cannot survive in honey, honey can support *Clostridium botulinum* endospores. In infants, the spores produce endospores in the small intestines and from there pass into the bloodstream. One fifth of infant botulism is attributed to honey. Soil is a much more common source. The disease is readily treated under clinical care. Infant mortality rate is less than one percent among hospitalized infant patients. Symptoms first manifest as weakness in the facial muscles that control chewing, swallowing, eye movement, and eyelid support. The weakness then spreads to the arms and legs and can eventually impair respiration. So: no honey for the baby!

For millennia, honey has been used for medical treatment. Modern analysis confirms that honey is antibacterial. Oonly in 2010 A.D. did scientists figure out why. The antibacterial component is a compound called defensin-1. The bees put it in there. It comes from their own immune system.

Anaphylaxis, or anaphylactic shock, is a severe allergic reaction to any of many substances, including goods, medications, and the venom of bees and wasps. A first exposure does not result in an allergic reaction, but any subsequent exposure can do so. Symptoms can include rash, itchiness, swelling of the tongue or throat, and a drop in blood pressure with a consequent quickening of the heart rate. Loss of consciousness may result. In the United States, 500-1,000 people die of anaphylaxis each year. Treatment is an injection of epinephrine into the thigh muscle, often with an autoinjector. EpiPen is a common brand. Injection is followed by a quickening of the heart rate, a rise in blood pressure, and a feeling of chilliness in the blood. Additional injections are often necessary. Immediate medical attention is essential.

Though there are no clinical studies to prove it, honey may alleviate allergies to pollen. The theory is that the small amounts of pollen in honey can trigger an immune response that produces antibodies that deal with pollen. After repeated doses, the body may become accustomed to the pollen and therefore might produce less histamine and thus experience less allergic reaction. Such honey treatment should be with raw honey that has not been pasteurized or filtered to remove "impurities." *Do not, however, give honey to an infant under the age of one. See the note on page 74 regarding honey and botulism in infants.*

Honey, being high in antioxidants, may prevent cellular damage in the brain. One study showed that menopausal women taking 20 grams of honey a day had better short-term memory than similar women taking hormone pills.

Honey also helps the body absorb calcium, which is something the brain needs to function properly. Honey may prevent or delay dementia, though there are no studies to prove it.

A 2010 study ("Effect of Honey on Nocturnal Cough and Sleep Quality...") found that honey was more effective than a placebo in reducing a persistent cough in children. In other words, honey was better than nothing. The childre in the study received ten grams of honey half an hour before bedtime.

Another study with children age two and up with upper respiratory infections found that two teaspoons of honey was just as effective as dextromethorphan, the common over-the-counter cough medicine. *Note, however, that due to a risk of infant botulism, a very serious food poisoning, honey should never be given to a child under the age of one.*

Can honey treat dandruff and hair loss? Here's the abstract from a study in the European Journal of Medical Research, "Therapeutic and prophylactic effects of crude honey on chronic seborrheic dermatitis and dandruff."

Honey has antibacterial, antifungal and antioxidant activities and has high nutrient value. In this study we investigated the potential use of topical application of crude honey in the management of seborrheic dermatitis and dandruff. Thirty patients with chronic seborrheic dermatitis of scalp, face and front of chest were entered for study. Twenty patients were males and 10 were females. Their ages ranged between 15 and 60 years. The patients had scaling, itching and hair loss. The lesions were scaling macules, papules and dry white plaques with crust and fissures. The patients were asked to apply diluted crude honey (90% honey diluted in warm water) every other day on the lesions with gentle rubbing for 2-3 minutes. Honey was left for 3 hours before gentle rinsing with warm water. The patients were followed daily for itching, scaling, hair loss, and the lesions were examined. Treatment was continued for 4 weeks. The improved patients were included in a prophylactic phase, lasting six months. Half of the patients were treated with the topical honey once weekly and the other half served as control. All the patients responded markedly with application of honey. Itching was relieved and scaling disappeared within one week. Skin lesions were healed and disappeared completely within 2 weeks. In addition, patients showed subjective improvement in hair loss. None of the patients (15 patients) treated with honey application once weekly for six months showed relapse while the 12/15 patients who had no prophylactic treatment with honey experienced a relapse of the lesions 2-4 months after stopping treatment. It might be concluded that crude honey could markedly improve seborrheic dermatitis and associated hair loss and prevent relapse when applied weekly.

Honey has also been found to help people sleep. It causes a rise in insulin and serotonin. Serotonin is a neurotransmitter that improves mood and happiness. The body converts serotonin into melatonin, which regulates sleep. Honey also contains tryptophan, the same soporific component found in turkey that results in sleepiness after a Thanksgiving meal. The body converts tryptophan into serotonin and then serotonin into melatonin. So why cook a turkey on Thanksgiving? Just have some honey!

A clinical review in the British Medical Journal, "Oesophagus: Heartburn and Honey," reported that honey can help prevent gastro-oesophageal reflux and may relieve heartburn.

In general, the darker the honey, the stronger its antibacterial and antioxidant power.

Aside from its nutritional value, honey is no better than white sugar or brown sugar for people on diets or people with diabetes. In terms of calories, the sugar part of honey has the same effects as cane sugar.

Beekeeping

Bees are the only domesticated insect and the only insect that produces food for humans. The closest thing to exceptions would be in cultures where people eat actual insects, such as ants and grasshoppers. There have also been flea circuses involving actual fleas trapped in harnesses. Ants have also been used for entertainment and observation purposes in "ant farm" toys. But bees are the only real insect farm animals.

Yao honeyhunters in modern Mozambique follow a wood-pecker-like bird known as the honeyguide. Honeyhunters and honeyguides communicate with each other as the bird leads the hunter to hives that are high in trees. The Yao, a Bantu Muslim people of southeast Africa, first recruit the birds by trilling *brrrrr* and then grunting *hmmm*. When the honeyguide finds a hive—easy for them thanks to their extra large olfactory bulb—it finds a Yao and flies low, singing a *Let's Go* song. The hunters follow the guide until it sings a *Here It Is* song and flicks its white tail. Then the hunters wrap dry wood in a banana leaf attached to the end of a long pole. Then they ignite leaf and wood and extend the pole up to the hive. Once the bees are smoked out, the hunters chop the tree down. The hunters get the honey and leave the wax for the bird. This is a rare case of wild animals helping humans hunt in return for payment.

The type of hive used by most modern beekeepers is called a Langstroth hive, named for its inventor, Lorenzo Lorraine Langstroth (1810-1895). Langstroth patented his invention in 1851. The hive design induces bees to build comb on frames that can be individually moved, removed, or replaced. The hives and frames are of standard measurement, making the parts interchangeable.

Typically a Langstroth hive has two brood chambers—two boxes each of which are 9-9/16 inches deep. Ten frames, 9 inches deep, hang from a rim near the top of the box. One brood chamber sits atop the other. This combined space is mostly dedicated to the laying of eggs and rearing of brood.

One or more supers sit atop the brood chambers. These medium-depth boxes, typically 6-5/8 inches deep, hold ten frames that are dedicated to the storage of honey.

A medium-depth frame holds about six pounds of honey. A deep frame from the brood chamber holds about eight pounds. A fully laden bee hive, in a good year, may weigh as much as a cubic meter of freshly fallen snow, two baby elephants, 30 full-grown Dachshunds, five toilets, or one-four-hundredth of the Space Shuttle.

Chimpanzees have been observed using tools to raid bee nests, but some in the Congo Basin are especially good at it. The use of hollow dipsticks to pull honey from a nest is fairly common. But Congo chimps have used clubs to pound on hives and sticks to lever open sealed nests. Congo chimps also rotate sticks to drill into nests and use strips of bark to scoop honey. They use leafy twigs to whisk or swat bees off themselves. They've also used sticks to dig up colonies in the ground. In that these skills seem to be regional, these technologies may be traditions passed on by communities. Traditions imply culture and even history—elements of humanity which may not be restricted to humans.

As of 2013, propolis is mentioned in 2,884 patents. The first patented use was in 1904. Incidence soared at the turn of the 21st century. China filed the most patents, followed by Japan, Korea, and Russia. About six percent of patents involving propolis are for dental treatments.

Brazil exported 91,979 pounds of propolis in 2012, with Japan its biggest buyer. Presumably most of it was the product of Africanized "killer bees," though that would make no difference in the quality of the product.

Marie Therese Bourgeois Chouteau, known as "la Mere de St. Louis" and said to be the first white woman to settle in Missouri, is reputed to have had the first honey bees brought to the territory. As the story goes, someone brought her a gift of a comb of honey from Illinois. She'd never known of the stuff, so she sent a trustworthy black man to find out the secret of it. He returned to report that it came from "a kind of fly." He brought back a box of the strange flies for her to raise. She became Missouri's first beekeeper.

Smoke pacifies bees by threatening an imminent danger of fire. The bees gorge on honey with the expectation of needing to fly it away to safety. Their full bellies make them a little sluggish and less aggressive. The smoke also masks the pheromones that bees release to alert their compatriots to danger.

According to the Food and Agriculture Organization of the U.N., the world is known to have produced 1,663,798 tons of honey in 2013. (An unknown additional quantity was produced in countries that did not report production.) China produced 450,300 tons of honey. The next biggest producers were Turkey (94,694 tons), Argentina (80,000 tons) and Ukraine (73,713 tons). The United States produced 67,812 tons. The Americas as a whole produced only 20 percent of the world's honey that year. Afghanistan produced 2,000 tons—not bad, considering.

To make a beard of bees, grab a queen from a hive and clip her to a man's beard. In short order, all the bees will leave the hive to come join her, draping themselves around her. Since they are not defending a hive at that point, they are nonaggressive. Still, removing the beard of bees can be a bit tricky. The queen must be located in the draping, writhing wad, unclipped without losing her, and returned to the hive, where her family will soon join her and see that she gets back to work.

In 2012, a dozen French beekeepers around the town of Ribeauville became understandably concerned when they found their bees producing honey in a variety of bright colors. They traced the color to a biogas plant that turned organic materials, including industrial waste, into methane. The plant, 2.5 miles away, was processing M&Ms, the little melt-in-your-mouth-not-in-your-hand candies from Mars company. Bees were eating the crunchy shells and bringing them home. While it might seem like a perfect opportunity to produce tutti-frutti honey candy, the contents were too questionable, so the honey had to be discarded.

Ethiopia has two million households that practice beekeeping as their primary livelihood. No single ethnic groupin Ehtiopia does not practice beekeeping. The nation produces the most honey of any African nation and ranks ninth in the world. It ranks third in the world in production of beeswax, after China and Mexico. Still, per-hive production is low, just 11-17 lbs. per year, perhaps because 90 percent of colonies are in "traditional" hives, tubes that do not use frames. Langstroth hives produce an average of over 72 lbs. per year. Eighty-five percent of the honey produced in Ethiopia is used to brew *tej*, a honey wine.

The USDA reports that over half of the honey sold in the U.S. is imported. In 2014 the country imported more than $547 million worth of honey. "Honey laundering" makes it difficult or impossible to determine where a given jar of honey comes from. Since sources are impossible to identify, much (an unknowable amount) of the imported honey is contaminated with sugars, heavy metals, or antibiotics.

Frequently Asked Questions

Q: Do bees have knees?

A: Bees have six jointed legs but no kneecaps, which basically means no knees.

Q: Can bees see color?

A: Bees can see better at the blue end of the spectrum, including ultraviolet light, which flowers tend to reflect. But bees can't see the color at the red end of the spectrum. They know a violet's violet but never suspect a rose is red. Sugar, they are sure, is sweet.

Q: How far can a honey bee fly?

A: No farther than necessary, but a really hungry honey bee can fly five miles to food.

Q: How high can a honey bee fly?

A: No higher than necessary to get over an obstacle. But a desperate drone on a mating flight will fly up over 250 feet for a shot at the queen. If successful, regardless of height, he will be dead before he hits the ground, his endophallus remaining with the queen.

Q: What should I do if I'm being chased by a swarm of bees?

A: The best thing to do is wake up. The bees will instantly vanish. In real life, a swarm of bees does not chase anyone. If you are being pestered by a lot of bees, you are probably near a hive. Walk away, slapping yourself as you go. If it's an actual swarm—a mass of thousands of bees flying in formation or hanging in a wad on a branch—they are in no mood to sting. They are looking for a home. Temporarily homeless, they have no home to defend and therefore no reason to sting. If you wait long enough, the swarm will go away. *Do not kill the swarm.* If you know a beekeeper, he or she will probably be very happy to come get the bees.

Q: Suppose there's a hive of honey bees living in the ground of my yard or making a nest under the eave of my house...what should I do?

A: Honey bees don't live in the ground or under eaves. If they're in the ground, they are probably yellow jackets. If they are under an eave in a papery nest, they are wasps. Neither yellow jackets nor wasps honey, and they sting without a lot of provocation. You'd best get rid of them. If they really are honey bees, call a bee-

98

keeper.

Q: What are the advantages of local honey?

A: There is a theory that local honey helps prevent allergies. This is scientifically unproven, but there are many anecdotal cases of people claiming beneficial effects. A good reason to buy local honey is that small-scale beekeepers respect their honey and their bees. They aren't likely to ruin the honey by boiling it or micro-filtering it. They probably don't add sugars to stretch it. Most honeys sold on an industrial scale have been boiled (to prevent it from crystallizing) or micro-filtered, which removes most of the elements that make honey honey. This is why "supermarket honey" tastes different from real, untreated honey. Another good reason to buy local honey is that beekeepers help bees survive, which helps the pollination of local plants.

Q: How can I become a highly respected member of my community?

A: Become a beekeeper. The best way to start is to find a beekeepers association. A quick search of the Internet or social media will probably turn up a few contacts. You'll also need a good book or two.

Q: What do I need to get started in beekeeping? How much does it cost?

A: You need a complete hive with frames for the bees to build comb on. That costs about $150. You will also need a package of bees. A package is a box with screens on two sides. They usually come with a queen in a small cage inside the package. Depending on where you live, a 3-lb. package costs around $75-$125. Prepare to start your beehive in the spring. A search of the Internet will turn up many companies that sell beekeeping equipment and others that sell packages of bees that can be ordered by mail or from a local distributor. In eastern Connecticut, that would be Stonewall Apiary in Hanover. (See ct-honey.com.) Stonewall Apiary ships honey and equipment but not bees, which have to be picked up on specific dates.

Q: Where's a good place for a beehive?

A: Outdoors. Shade would be nice in a place of brutal sun. Under a linden tree would be heaven to bees. Don't worry about the bees bothering people. Worry about people bothering the bees. Note that you will need to be able to prevent vegetation from blocking the entrance.

Installing Bee Packages

A bee package consists of three pounds of bees in a box with screen on two sides. You want to install those bees as soon as you get them. You can see the bees in there, eager to get out and get back to normal life. You can also see a can in there, hanging from the top. It's full of sugar water from which the bees have been sipping through little holes in the bottom. Beside the can hangs the queen cage, a little box the size of a clumsy carpenter's thumb.

(If you have received a queen only, without a package, to replace an old queen, the instructions are basically the same. Just make sure there is no queen in the hive or the new queen and the resident queen will end up fighting until one of the two is dead. If there's still an old queen in the hive, find her, thank her for her service, then behead her and leave her body outside the hive near the entrance so her loyal subjects get the message.)

The queen is in a cage because she is not the natural, original queen of the bees she is with. The bees in the package still see her as an intruder. If she weren't in a cage, they'd kill her. The complication of installing a package of bees is the process of not releasing the queen until she's accepted as one of the gang. Here's how:

1. Take the package to a hive that is all set up and ready to go, including a feeder with sugar water. A pollen patty would be good, too. This hive should be just a single brood chamber, or, better, a nuc (short for "nucleus," a small hive with only five frames). A nuc's smaller size makes it easier for a small swarm to keep itself warm. Remove the top from the hive or nuc. Remove the inner cover. Remove a frame from the middle of the set of frames. Ideally, this frame will have comb on it. (Beg or buy a few frames with comb from another beekeeper. It will help a lot because the queen will immediately have somewhere to lay eggs.) In the upper part of the comb, in the corner that will be at the back of the hive, carve out a vertical space big enough for a queen cage, about an inch wide and three inches long. If the frame has no comb, see below.

2. Now it's time to get the queen cage out of the package. Pry up the flat piece of wood at the top of the package. See the can. See the silvery disk next to it. From that disk hangs the queen cage. If you pull it up, bees will start flowing up through the hole, each and every one of them in a bad mood. If you fail to prevent that, you'll be in a bad mood, too. So give the package a solid thump on the ground or the top of the hive. The bees will fall to the bottom of the box in a mass of confusion. This will give you a few seconds to pull up the queen cage and quickly set the flat piece of wood

back over the hole before bees come flying out.

3. Look at that queen! Isn't she beautiful? She's long, slender and tan, like a girl from Ipanema with six legs, diaphanous wings, and a spermatheca ready to go. Look at her wiggle in there with her comfort maids. If the queen isn't wiggling, you've got yourself a dead queen and a real problem. Call a beekeeper or the jerk who sold you the bees. You need a queen, and quick.

4. There are two ends to the queen cage, each with a short tunnel capped with a tiny cork. You can't see the cork on one side because of the silvery disk that is nailed over it. Pull that disk off. Now you can see how one tunnel is packed with a white candy. The idea is, the queen and her attendants are going to start eating her way through that tunnel while the bees outside start eating their way in. By the time they meet, the queen and the bees will have been in the hive long enough to become friends. The drones, of course, will be going absolutely nuts. So pull the cork out of the candy tunnel. Leave the other cork in place! It's an emergency exit. We'll get to that.

5. Nestle that queen cage into the place you carved in the comb. Best to put the candy tunnel facing up. This is so that if a bee dies inside the cage, her body doesn't block the tunnel. Set the cage so that the screened part faces the inside of the hive. This is so the bees can see and tend to

104

their queen. Carefully set the frame back in place in the hive. Give the bees a pollen patty to help them produce comb. Put the inner cover on.

6. Now's the part where you might get stung. Once again, thump the package on the ground (not on the hive) so all the bees tumble down again. Now you've got a few seconds to pull that can out of its hole. This can be tricky. You'll need your hive tool or knife blade and some fingernails to pull it up far enough to get your ungloved fingers around it. Pull it up. Slap the wooden top over the hole. Did you get stung? Well, too bad. You're a beekeeper. What were you expecting? Utter the curse of your choice, pull the stinger out, and move on.

7. Now to let the bees go into the hive. Thump them down to the bottom of the package. Remove the wooden top and lay the box upside down on the inner cover so that the feeding–can hole is over the inner cover hole. Now the bees' only way out is into the hive, which is surely where they will go. It might take them an hour or two to make the move, but they'll like it in there. It smells good, there's some sugar water, it's nice and dark, and there's a queen who ain't bad lookin' even if she still smells a little funny. Why go anywhere else?

8. Go get something to sit on and a beer, unless you're a Mormon, many of whom are beekeepers, and for good rea-

sons. They and other teetotalers might appreciate a lemonade at this wonderful moment. Have a seat near the front of the hive. Drink your chosen beverage. You deserve it. You're a beekeeper, and you've just done the world a favor.

9. Before dark, put the hive cover back on. Leave that hive alone for three days. After that, puff a bit of smoke in the entrance and gently, furtively, pull off the top and inner cover. Check to see if the queen got out. If she didn't, pop the cork from the emergency exit and put the cage back. If she's out, you can assume she's doing her business. Remove the empty queen cage and close up the hive. Go read a book about beekeeping and see what you have to do next.

Information, Equipment, Supplies, Bees

Beekeeping Suppliers

Better Bee
Greenwich, NY
betterbee.com
800-632-3379

Brushy Mountain Bee Farm
Home office in Moravian Falls, NC.
brushymountainbeefarm.com
800-233-7929

Mann Lake
Hackensack, MN
mannlakeltd.com
800-880-7694

Dadant
Home office in Hamilton, IL
dadant.com
888-922-1293 plus branches in 10 states

Stonewall Apiary
Hanover, CT
ct-honey.com

Packaged Bees

Bees can be ordered through the U.S. Postal Service, but the USPS is often slow, so many (or even all) bees die along the way. You may need to order them months in advance. Some suppliers will not ship during hot months. To find suppliers, search the internet for "bee packages." If possible, buy bees from local suppliers in the spring. In Connecticut and Rhode Island, Stonewall Apiary (ct-honey. com) is a good supplier.

Books on Beekeeping

Backyard Beekeeper, by Kim Flottum

The Beekeeper's Handbook, by Diana Sammataro

Top-Bar Beekeeping: Organic Practices for Honeybee Health, by Les Crowder

Storey's Guide to Keeping Honey Bees, by Malcom T. Sanford and Richard E. Bonney

The Complete Idiot's Guide to Beekeeping, by Dean Stiglitz and Laurie Herboldsheimer

Acknowledgements

The artwork on the front and back covers was contributed by Colleen Hennessy (the flowers) and Kathleen Boushee (the bees). Special thanks also go to New London Librarium editors Ralph Hunter Cheney, Denise Dembinski, and Richard Waterman.

About the Author

Hezekiah Jamoke is a heteronymic writer created by Glenn Alan Cheney, a writer, editor, translator, publisher, retired beekeeper, and jamoke of all trades. He has written books on nuns, Lincoln, Brazil, Chernobyl, Central America, drug addiction, the Pilgrims, and several other topics as well as smatterings of fiction, poetry, translations, and essays.